WHO? WHAT? WHY?

WHO IS DONALD TRUMP?

JULIA ADAMS

WAYLAND

www.waylandbooks.co.uk

First published in Great Britain in 2017 by Wayland

ISBN 978 1 5263 0687 6

10 9 8 7 6 5 4 3 2 1

Wayland
An imprint of
Hachette Children's Group
Part of Hodder & Stoughton
Carmelite House
50 Victoria Embankment
London EC4Y 0DZ

An Hachette UK Company
www.hachette.co.uk
www. hachettechildrens.co.uk

A catalogue for this title is available from the British Library.

Printed in China.

Produced for Wayland
by White-Thomson Publishing Ltd
www.wtpub.co.uk
Editor: Julia Adams
Designer: Dan Prescott, Couper Street Type Co.

Picture acknowledgements:
Cover, p. 1, p. 34: Evan El-Amin/Shutterstock; p. 3: jctabb/Shutterstock; p. 4: Ashraf Shazly/Stringer/Getty Images; p. 5 (top): Ken Wolter/Shutterstock; p. 5 (bottom): Evan El-Amin/Shutterstock; p. 6 (centre): Ron Galella/Getty Images; p. 6 (bottom): Eric Urquhart/Shutterstock; p. 7: Tinseltown/Shutterstock; p. 8: Evan E-Amin/Shutterstock; p. 9: Mike Coppola/Getty Images; p. 10: Charlie Archambault/Alamy Live News; p. 11: Ken Wolter/Shutterstock; p. 12: Valery Sharifulin/TASS/Alamy Live; p. 13 (Democrat logo): tony4urban/Shutterstock; p. 13 (Republican logo): Skunkeye/Shutterstock; p. 14: Joseph Sohm/Shutterstock; p. 15: Pool/Getty Images; p. 16 (top): Boston Globe/Getty Images; p. 16 (infographic logos): Puckung/Shutterstock; p. 17 (top icon): Marina9/Shutterstock; p. 17 (centre icon): eatcute/Shutterstock; p. 17 (bottom icon): alexwhite/Shutterstock; p. 18: Barbara Kalbfleisch/Shutterstock; p. 19: Dan Callister/Alamy Stock Photo; p. 21: Win McNamee/Getty Images; p. 22: amadeustx/Shutterstock; p. 23: Scott London/AlamyStock Photo; p. 24: Nicole S Glass/Shutterstock; p. 25: chrisdorney/Shutterstock; p. 27: Mark Reinstein/Getty Images; p. 28: JStone/Shutterstock; p. 29 (top): Tim Sloane/Getty Images; p. 29 (bottom): lev radin/Shutterstock; p. 30: The Washington Post/Getty Images; p. 32: Alex Wong/Getty Images; p. 33: lev radin/Shutterstock; p. 35: a katz/Shutterstock; p. 36: Jim West/Alamy Stock Photo; p. 37: ITAR/TASS Photo Agency/Alamy Live News; p. 38: Cheriss May/NurPhoto/Getty Images; p. 39: ID1974/Shutterstock; p. 40: Diego G Diaz/Shutterstock; p. 41: Jim Lambert/Shutterstock; p. 42: WAYHOME Studio/Shutterstock; p. 43: turtix/Shutterstock; p. 44: Rob Crandall/Shutterstock; p. 45: Cynthia Johnson/Getty Images; p. 47: Lima Junior/Shutterstock.
All backgrounds and design elements: Shutterstock.

Every attempt has been made to clear copyright. Should there be any inadvertent omission please apply to the publisher for rectification.

The website addresses (URLs) included in this book were valid at the time of going to press. However, it is possible that contents or addresses may have changed since the publication of this book. No responsibility for any such changes accepted by either the author or the publisher.

CONTENTS

WHY IS DONALD TRUMP SO IMPORTANT?

On 8 November 2016, some 130 million people in the USA cast their vote to decide who should become their next President. The candidates, Hillary Clinton and Donald Trump, had fought a campaign that had divided their country more than any previous election. And the resulting Trump presidency would not only affect the citizens of the USA, but billions of people around the world.

WORLD LEADER

The President of the United States is often referred to as a 'world leader'. He or she governs a country that is both one of the richest and most powerful in the world. Decisions made during each administration affect how much money is spent on international aid, where military troops are deployed, commitments to the environment and climate change, and where trade is established. So even though the President is voted for in the USA, his or her actions are felt globally, and can have an impact on billions of lives.

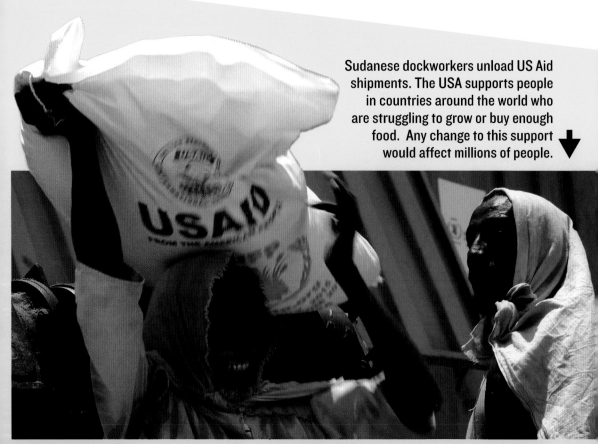

Sudanese dockworkers unload US Aid shipments. The USA supports people in countries around the world who are struggling to grow or buy enough food. Any change to this support would affect millions of people.

A CONTROVERSIAL CHOICE?

Donald Trump is in many ways a unique choice for President – he is a businessman, rather than a politician. He has never held a job in government or the military. His supporters welcome this as a fresh perspective, and believe that Trump will bring about the change to government that they are hoping to see. Opponents, though, are fearful that Trump's inexperience may lead to poor decisions and ultimately endanger the well-being of the US and global population.

Donald Trump owns 17 golf clubs around the world, including properties in Dubai and Scotland.

THE FULL PICTURE

Whether people agree with Trump's election and policies or not, he is a leader who has already had a big impact on politics and political activism around the world. He has created controversy in global politics and through his use of social media. He divides opinions and is in many ways an unusual figure in the history of the US presidency. In this book, we aim to give the full, balanced picture of who Trump is – his background, how he became President, what he has done so far as leader of the United States, and where his journey may take him.

Trump holding an event for his supporters, marking 100 days of his presidency.

WHO IS DONALD J. TRUMP?

On 20 January 2017, Donald J. Trump was sworn into office as 45th President of the United States. He is the first President in history to enter the White House with no political or military qualifications. His campaign was controversial, and he won contrary to many predictions and expectations. His election has divided opinion more sharply than any other in US history. So who is Donald Trump?

FAMILY BUSINESS

Donald John Trump was born in 1946 as the fourth of five children to Mary MacLeod and Frederick Trump. He grew up in Queens, New York, and took over his father's real-estate (property) business after graduating from the University of Pennsylvania. He re-named the company The Trump Organization, and became known for his extravagant projects – lavish buildings worth millions of dollars, often named after him. His most famous is Trump Tower, a 58-storey building on 5th Avenue in New York that houses an 18-metre waterfall.

↑ Donald Trump and his father, Fred, in 1987.

← Trump Tower in New York City, USA. The building is 58 storeys high, although Trump claims that its top floor is the 68th.

CAREER AND TV FAME

Trump experienced a series of successes and failures as a businessman. Some of his companies have made millions of dollars, but on the other hand, six of them had to file for bankruptcy, and he has been sued by many people over his business practices. He has owned casinos, hotels, luxury apartments, beauty contests and a private business school. Most recently, he was the star of the reality TV show *The Apprentice*, in which contestants compete to be hired by Trump. Trump hosted the series from 2004 until 2015, and it was one of the most watched TV shows in the USA.

Trump filming at Universal Studios for the sixth season of *The Apprentice* in 2006.

THE POLITICAL WORLD

Trump first made a name for himself in politics when he started the 'birther movement', which tried to discredit President Obama by wrongly claiming that he hadn't been born in the USA. Despite Obama releasing his birth certificate, proving that he was born in the US state of Hawaii, Trump persisted. He took to Twitter to criticise President Obama during his years in office, and his tweets attracted many followers. In 2015, Trump announced he was running for President.

EARLY CONTROVERSIES

Once Trump had announced that he was going to run for the US presidency, he began to make regular public appearances. While his fans turned out in large numbers, cheering him on and praising this new voice in politics, Trump also attracted an unusual amount of criticism. Many strongly disapproved of the way he dealt with protesters who appeared at his events, by demanding that they be removed. In some cases, members of the crowd saw this as an encouragement to inflict violence on the protestors. In one such instance, Trump was later sued for inciting a violent attack.

SEPT 2016 Presidential candidate Trump holds a speech at a campaign rally in Pennsylvania.

RACISM

As the campaign trail continued, Trump's events attracted attention for other controversial issues, too. Reports described some crowd members at rallies chanting racist slurs, without Trump denouncing them. Trump's speeches became more outspoken about immigration, particularly from the USA's neighbour, Mexico. He characterised many Mexicans crossing the border to the USA as being criminals. He spoke negatively about the Muslim community, claiming that, as President, he would close down the borders to stop Muslim travellers from entering the country.

TRUMP AND WOMEN

Much of the criticism levelled at Trump has related to his treatment of women. He has a history of being sued by women for sexual assault, and during the campaign this also became an issue. Trump claimed that all these women were lying. A video from 2005 that was leaked during the campaign revealed Trump boasting about sexually assaulting women; in it, he also claimed that his status and wealth meant women let him do 'anything' to them. The recording caused an outcry among both his opponents and his supporters. His defence was that he wasn't being serious, and that this should be treated as banter. His wife, Melania, stated that she forgave him.

Attorney Gloria Allred speaks during the Women Seeking Justice Against Trump press conference. She is flanked by women who have accused Trump of sexual harassment.

BEING TRUMP

Trump has written various books that offer some insight into his personality. In 1987, Donald Trump wrote the book *The Art of the Deal*, together with the writer Tony Schwartz. In it, Trump describes how he became a successful businessman by aggressively striking big, bold deals and gaining huge publicity in the process. There are many parallels between his business style and the way he ran his presidential campaign. He created controversy, told people what they wanted to hear and had a deep mistrust of the media. Supporters are hopeful that Trump's confident style of getting the best deal possible will mean that he will do the same for the USA as its President. Opponents, on the other hand, are deeply concerned that Trump's unconventional approach to business will mean he misuses or at least misjudges his presidential power.

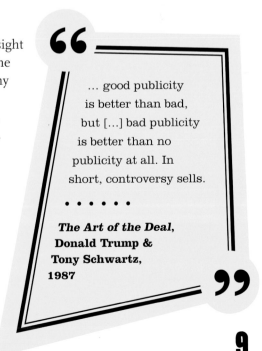

" ... good publicity is better than bad, but [...] bad publicity is better than no publicity at all. In short, controversy sells.

• • • • • •

The Art of the Deal, Donald Trump & Tony Schwartz, 1987

"

JAN 2017 President Donald Trump, having just delivered his inaugural address, greets the crowds together with his Vice President, Mike Pence (left). His wife, Melania, looks on (right, second row).

THE NEW PRESIDENT

On being sworn in as 45th President of the United States, Trump delivered an inaugural speech that promised to place the USA before all other countries. He focused on building up the USA and strengthening its borders, repeating many of his campaign promises. Around him, his wife Melania, politicians and supporters proceeded to congratulate the new world leader. They believed he would change the USA for the better. But beyond the celebrations, thousands of people were taking to the streets in protest. Both in Washington DC, where the inauguration was taking place, and in the rest of the USA, Trump's opponents had one overriding message: he was not their President.

A ROCKY START

Various news outlets took photographs of the crowd attending the Trump inauguration and discovered that it was visibly smaller than at the last Obama inauguration. The new White House administration claimed attendance numbers had been faked by the media – a claim that was repeatedly shown to be untrue. Despite clear evidence, the White House Press Secretary stated that the crowd was the largest that had ever attended an inauguration. Newspapers also reported that a number of protesters who had been arrested could be given prison sentences, which is unusually harsh for the USA. It looked as if Trump and his staff were trying very hard to push back against the negative attention.

THE WOMEN'S MARCH

On Trump's first full day in office, a global movement called Women's March staged coordinated protests in towns and cities all over the world. Between three and four million people took part in order to voice their opposition to Trump becoming President. They took issue with the new leader's history of alleged sexual assault and his general attitude towards women. They believed that he wasn't going to represent women's interests and defend their rights. Based on Trump's campaign, they believed that ethnic minorities, LGBTI people, disabled people and people of non-Christian beliefs were vulnerable under the new President as well. The protest was the largest in the history of the USA.

Given people's reactions, how was it possible for someone as controversial as Trump to become the President of the USA?

Millions of people attended the Women's March protests around the world on 21 January 2017. In many cases, such as St Paul, USA, the protests were some of the biggest in the city's history.

JAN 2017

WHY IS DONALD TRUMP THE PRESIDENT OF THE USA?

In the United States, the President is the leader of the country, and is supported by their staff and the Vice President. Because the USA is a democracy, the President is voted for by the people. The idea of a democracy is that the people of a country decide who should lead them. Each democracy may have a different way of voting for their leader and other representatives.

POLITICAL PARTIES

Most people who run for President in the USA belong to a political party. Parties are groups of people who agree on how they think the country should be run. They use manifestos to present their policies to voters. Parties are often broadly described as being 'right', 'centre' or 'left'. These terms are used to sum up the attitude a party has to key political issues – they are the party's ideology. In the USA, there are two main parties: the Republicans and the Democrats. The Republicans are described as 'right', or 'conservative', while the Democrats are considered 'left', or 'liberal'.

THIRD PARTIES

While the Republican and the Democrat parties win the majority of the votes in the USA, there are other parties whose members run for office, too. Some people run for President as independent candidates – they don't belong to any party and have their own manifesto; the Libertarian party, the Green party, the Reform party and the Constitution party are so-called 'third parties' who are active in US politics. However, none of their representatives has ever been voted President.

Jill Stein of the Green Party was the presidential candidate for the 2012 and the 2016 elections.

IDEOLOGIES OF REPUBLICANS AND DEMOCRATS:

Democrats:

Republicans:

Founded: 1828

Main ideology: government should be strong, there should be equal opportunities for everyone, no matter what their background is, and the state should provide for those in need. This is funded by people paying tax, according to their income.

Founded: 1854

Main ideology: government should be limited, there should be individual freedom and low tax, and people should be encouraged to make their own fortune, rather than having much support from the state. Republicans support a strong military defence.

TRUMP'S POLITICS

As President of the United States, Donald Trump is representing the Republican party. But he hasn't always sided with the Republicans. From the 1980s onwards, his political opinions and affiliations have changed a number of times – he has supported the Republican party, the Democrat party, the Reform party, and considered running as an independent candidate for the 2012 presidential election. His political opinions have varied greatly over the years and depending on the topic, which has lead some journalists to say it is impossible to fully understand his political beliefs.

THE RACE BEGINS

The President of the United States is voted on every four years by the country's citizens who are 18 or over. Anyone can stand for election, provided they were born in the USA, are at least 35 years old, and have lived in the country for at least 14 years. This sometimes means that at the beginning of the race to the White House, there are many candidates competing. For the 2016 elections, 23 candidates started campaigning about two years before the election.

CAMPAIGNING

Candidates use campaign events, such as rallies and speeches, to try and attract voters. They tour the country to get as much publicity as they can, in order to let people know what they stand for and what their intended policies are. Campaigns need to be very well organised, and involve a lot of people who work to raise money for their candidate. Campaigning is expensive, and each candidate needs to make sure enough money is raised on their behalf. The money is needed to organise events, pay staff and travel costs, produce campaign websites and organise phone banks. The total costs for all candidates in the run-up to the 2016 election was over US$2 billion.

Clinton speaks at a campaign rally in California. **JUNE 2016**

hillaryclinton.com
Fighting for us

PRIMARIES AND CAUCUSES

The first election the candidates face is the one that decides who is going to represent each party in the presidential elections. Members of each party get to vote in local events called caucuses or primaries. These elections decide which delegate will represent party members at the party's national convention. The national convention for each party takes place in the summer, a few months before the presidential election. At the convention, each delegate then votes to choose the presidential nominee – the person who will run for President for their party.

SEPT 2016

Donald Trump and Hillary Clinton during their first TV debate.

THE FINAL SPRINT

Now that the nominees are decided, campaigns become very focused on debates and differences between these two or three people. This includes TV debates, where nominees are asked how they plan to handle important issues, should they become President. TV debates have become very important, and the media often try to work out which candidate 'won' the debate. Then campaigning draws to a close, and the whole nation casts their vote on the first Tuesday in November.

THE ELECTORAL COLLEGE

When the US public vote, they don't directly vote for the person they want to be President. Based on the outcome of the popular vote in each state, electors are selected to represent them. The electors from all states form an electoral college. These 538 electors vote on who should be the next President of the United States. A candidate needs at least 270 of the electors' votes to win the presidential race. As it is clear from the beginning who each elector supports, the winner of the presidential election can be announced on election night. The electoral college vote to confirm the outcome of the presidential election then takes place in December; these votes are counted in early January. Even though a small number of electors may decide to vote differently from their initial choice, this has never changed the outcome of an election.

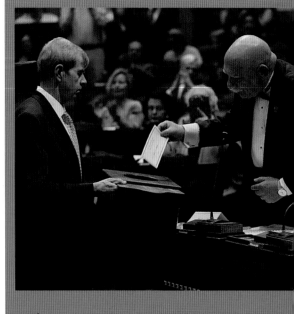

↑ An elector for Massachusetts casts his vote for the 2016 presidential election.

UNEVEN REPRESENTATION
· · · · · · · · · · · · · ·

WYOMING	CALIFORNIA
586,107	39.2 MILLION
VOTERS	VOTERS
3 ELECTORS	55 ELECTORS
195,369 NEEDED TO GAIN ONE ELECTORAL COLLEGE VOTE	711,724 NEEDED TO GAIN ONE ELECTORAL COLLEGE VOTE

FAIR REPRESENTATION?

Currently, the US President isn't voted in by a popular majority – it's not at all guaranteed that the person with the most votes from the public also wins the election. This is because the number of electors for each state doesn't always correspond to the number of people who live and vote there. On average, an elector represents about 436,000 people; however, in Wyoming, for example, an elector represents 195,369 citizens. So it takes far fewer votes to select an elector to represent their interests in the electoral college vote. Which is why some candidates have managed to win the popular vote (most people voted for them), but because of where each voter lived and how they were represented by their elector, the candidate lost the electoral college all the same.

THE 2016 NOMINEES

Of the two major parties, there were six Democrats and 17 Republicans who started out campaigning for the 2016 presidential elections. But after the primaries and national conventions, the two presidential candidates who everyone focused on were Hillary Clinton (for the Democrats) and Donald Trump (representing the Republicans). They stood for very different policies and their backgrounds were vastly different, too. Clinton has had a life-long career in politics, including her role as a very active First Lady when her husband, Bill Clinton, was President 1993–2001. In 2000, she was elected senator for New York State, and she then went on to serve as Secretary of State under Barack Obama. Trump, on the other hand, had been a businessman and not held any office in government before he ran for President.

KEY POLICIES

Environment:

Clinton – invest in renewable energy and reduce the USA's oil dependency by one-third

Trump – climate change is a hoax; increase use of fossil fuels and cut funding to the Environmental Agency

Immigration:

Clinton – create a pathway for immigrants to become citizens; abolish some forms of immigrant detention

Trump – build a wall along the Mexican border that Mexico will pay for; deport 11 million undocumented immigrants

Healthcare:

Clinton – keep Obamacare (see page 35); women should continue to get access to contraception and safe, legal abortion

Trump – replace Obamacare on day one; not clear on issues of women's health – campaign statements were the opposite of his manifesto

RALLYING FOR SUPPORT

Both Clinton and Trump had been campaigning for months before they were elected as presidential candidates for their parties. They each had strong support, and their events were attended by large crowds. In the months that followed, the USA witnessed a bitterly fought campaign that split the nation into Trump supporters and Clinton supporters with very little tolerance or understanding for each other. The USA was described as 'polarised' – consisting of two opposites, with no middle ground. The campaigns started to mirror this state of the nation, and more so than in previous elections, the tone at events was 'us versus them'.

"LOCK HER UP!"

Trump regularly alleged Clinton was a criminal, calling her 'crooked Hillary'. During the campaign, Clinton was investigated twice by the FBI due to the way she had used her email account while she served as Secretary of State. Both investigations concluded that Clinton hadn't committed anything unlawful. Nevertheless, Trump used these investigations as 'proof' that Clinton had something to hide, and couldn't be trusted. At some rallies, and even at the Republican national convention, crowds chanted 'Lock her up!', demanding that Clinton be imprisoned. Trump himself claimed that if he became President, he would see to her being jailed.

Many Trump voters believed Hillary Clinton was a criminal, and would often mock her at Trump rallies.

FAKE NEWS

During the campaign, it was not only Trump who spread false claims at his rallies and interviews. Globally, there was a sharp rise in 'fake news' – claims, articles and figures that were presented as facts, but were in reality false and misleading. The Internet, and especially social media, were often used to spread fake news, and in the USA, there was a noticeable amount of negative fake news about Hillary Clinton. It became troubling that people who were going to vote were being misinformed, and it was a challenge to debunk myths. For one, they spread incredibly quickly; and as a rumour, they caused suspicion, even if they were proven wrong.

CYBER ATTACK

Once the election was over, government officials confirmed that part of the rise in fake news was due to an active interference in the election. Russian hackers, sometimes referred to as 'Russian WikiLeaks', had targeted the Clinton campaign with fake news items and videos, in order to support Trump's team. Evidence indicated that these hackers had been supported by the Russian government.

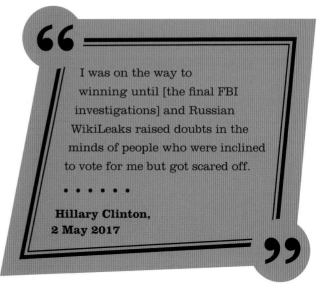

> I was on the way to winning until [the final FBI investigations] and Russian WikiLeaks raised doubts in the minds of people who were inclined to vote for me but got scared off.

Hillary Clinton, 2 May 2017

ELECTION NIGHT

On Tuesday 8 November 2016, campaigning had come to an end, and it was time for the USA to choose their next President. Despite the setbacks that Hillary Clinton had experienced during her campaign, most people expected her to win – she was a career politician and a household name. But as the night wore on, more and more states were declared for Donald Trump, and Clinton's win became increasingly unlikely. At 2 a.m. on Wednesday 9 November, Donald Trump was declared the winner of the presidential election. Despite almost 3 million more people voting for Clinton, Trump won with 306 electoral votes to Clinton's 232. Democrat voters were in deep shock; Trump voters were ecstatic.

NOV 2016 Trump is joined on stage by his family as he declares his victory in the 2016 presidential election.

HOW DID THIS HAPPEN?

For weeks after the election, journalists and many voters tried to understand how Trump could have won the presidential election. Both campaigns had struggled with controversies, but while many of the accusations made against Clinton were proved wrong, Trump remains accused of sexual assault as well as tolerating aggression and racism at his rallies. So when Trump won the election despite these circumstances, it became very important to understand who Trump's voters were.

WHO VOTED FOR TRUMP?

Many of the people who voted for Trump wanted to see a change, and felt forgotten by politicians. Often these were people who were struggling to find work, living in areas where there is a lot of poverty. There are whole areas of the USA that were built around industries that are no longer around. One example is a region called the Rust Belt. This area used to be called the Factory Belt, because it was the home of most of the USA's manufacturing industries. Whole towns and neighbourhoods were built up around factories. But in the twentieth century, a lot of these industries died, so people lost their jobs and many moved away. People who live in these deserted areas today are still struggling to find work, and believe politicians don't care about them. They saw Trump as the answer to their struggle. Many of these people are white working-class men who had traditionally voted Democrat.

2016 ELECTION RESULTS IN THE RUST BELT

Wisconsin
Michigan
New York
Pennsylvania
Indiana
Ohio
Illinois
West Virginia

Trump majority
Clinton majority
Rust Belt

WOMEN FOR TRUMP

Despite Trump's insulting remarks about women, and his lawsuits for sexual harassment, there were still a lot of women who voted for him. They did so for many different reasons. Some said that while they disagreed with Trump's attitude towards women, they still liked his politics. Others voted for him because the investigations into Clinton's email use made them distrust her, despite the fact that the FBI found no wrongdoing.

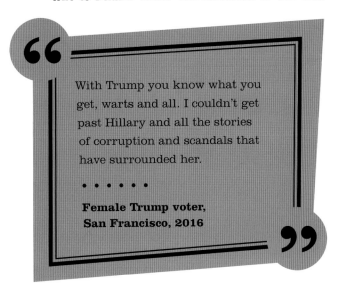

" With Trump you know what you get, warts and all. I couldn't get past Hillary and all the stories of corruption and scandals that have surrounded her.

• • • • • •

Female Trump voter, San Francisco, 2016 "

TRANSITION

While the new President of the United States gets elected in November, they are only sworn in in January. From election night until inauguration, both the sitting President and the President Elect conduct a transition period. During this time, the incoming and outgoing teams meet and discuss current issues, as well as basic facts about working (and living) in the White House. The President Elect also begins appointing staff and filling important positions. Trump's first visit to the

White House as President Elect was on 10 November, two days after the election. Reports by journalists stated that Trump didn't seem to understand some of the basics of how the US government works. He was reportedly surprised at how many tasks a President carries out every day in order to run the country. These reports began to worry people – would Donald Trump be up to the job?

Obama and Trump hold a press conference during the President Elect's first visit to the White House.

WHAT DOES THE PRESIDENT OF THE USA DO?

The President of the United States is the leader of the country. During their time in office, they and their family live in the White House in the USA's capital city, Washington DC. The President and his or her key staff also work in the White House, in a part called the West Wing.

WHERE THE PRESIDENT WORKS

The President's main office is called the Oval Office. Here, they will sign important documents, hold meetings and make phone calls to foreign leaders. The West Wing is the workplace of about 450 top advisors and assistants to the President. Other people who work for the White House have their offices close by, in one of the executive office buildings. Not far from the White House is the Capitol, where elected members of Congress meet.

WHITE HOUSE STATS

COMPLETED IN 1800

NUMBER OF ROOMS: 132

NUMBER OF BATHROOMS: 35

NUMBER OF FIREPLACES: 28

NUMBER OF FLOORS: 6

The White House gets redecorated with each new President, which also includes the Oval Office.

PRESIDENTIAL LEGACY

Trump is the 45th person to become President of the United States of America. Before him, a long history of leaders each sought to shape the country they knew into something better. They each had a vision for the USA, and worked hard to realise it. The first President of the United States was George Washington, who was inaugurated in 1789. He played a major role in writing the Constitution (see page 26) and was known for uniting people to work towards a common cause. He also commissioned the White House, which was completed when the second President, John Adams, was in office. From then on, first families have always lived and worked here.

HOW IMPORTANT IS THE PRESIDENT?

The role of President is very influential, and has the power to bring about changes to laws and rights, shaping the country's history and how it is run. For example, Harry S. Truman, the 33rd President of the United States, founded the CIA in 1947. He also approved the use of two atomic bombs to end the war with Japan in August 1945. John F. Kennedy is famed for ending the Cuban Missile Crisis, which could have resulted in a nuclear war. In 1964, Lyndon B. Johnson signed the Civil Rights Act, which ended the institutional segregation of people according to their race, and banned employment discrimination on the basis of race, colour, religion, gender or nationality. Four Presidents and one Vice President have received the Nobel Peace Prize. The role of US President comes with great responsibilities, but also huge opportunities to make a change.

Obama receiving his Nobel Peace Prize in 2009. The Nobel committee praised his focus on cooperation between peoples and his vision of a world without nuclear weapons.

A DAY IN THE LIFE OF A PRESIDENT

Each President has a routine that they like to stick to, but that aside, there are certain meetings and briefings that always need to be attended. On an average day, the President will receive the daily briefing from the National Security Advisor, take phone calls from leaders of other states, have meetings with White House staff and leaders from Congress, meet and greet people touring the White House, hold talks with visiting world leaders, sometimes talk to the press and retire at the end of the working day (around 6 p.m.) to spend time with their family.

PRESIDENT TRUMP'S DAY

President Obama used to spend time with his family in the mornings, before his daughters went to school, as well as having family dinner in the evenings. He then usually worked late into the night after dinner.

Before his wife and son came to live with him in the White House, Trump started the day by watching shows on cable news networks, such as Fox and MSNBC. He then read the papers (the *New York Times*, the *Washington Post* and the *New York Post*) and had breakfast, before heading to his first meeting, which was usually at 9 a.m.. The rest of the day was spent in and out of meetings and briefings, similar to his predecessors. In the evening, after leaving the West Wing, he returned to watching cable news shows. He is known to only sleep for about four hours at night, rising again at six in the morning.

Trump welcomes the Chancellor of Germany, Angela Merkel, to the White House in March 2017.

TRUMP ON TWITTER

One element that features heavily in Trump's day is his unprecedented use of the social media platform Twitter. He mostly uses his personal account (@realDonaldTrump), and his tweets are never filtered through his advisors. As a result, Trump has caused issues with foreign relations and ongoing investigations as well as creating confusion by contradicting White House statements. Nevertheless, Trump enjoys using this direct link to the public, and he uses it daily. His supporters love what they see as honest communication from the President, as they feel it makes him more accessible. Critics are concerned that an unfiltered line of communication may mean that the President says something damaging. But Trump has continued using Twitter as a key tool in his presidency, and his former Press Secretary, Sean Spicer, announced on 6 June 2017 that any Trump tweets are to be 'considered official statements by the President of the United States'.

Trump's Twitter page. Even though there is an official Twitter handle for the President of the United States (@POTUS), Trump prefers to use his private account for his presidential tweets.

THE CONSTITUTION

When America was declared an independent state in 1776, a committee of politicians drafted a document called the Constitution. In it, they set out what the President of the United States could do, how they should be elected, and later, through amendments, what rights citizens of the USA have, by birth. The Constitution remains the set of laws by which politicians, and especially the President, govern. When the President is sworn in, they declare to 'preserve, protect and defend the Constitution of the United States'. Their main job is to make decisions that are in the interest of the US people and are ethically sound.

HOW DOES THE PRESIDENT RULE?

The President isn't the only person who runs the country. To make sure that they don't have too much power, and, more importantly, they don't misuse their power, or behave unconstitutionally, the US government is set up as a system of 'checks and balances'. This means that no one person has too much power – decisions are checked by other elected officials, and everyone has the duty to make sure that the laws that get passed and the decisions that get made are constitutional.

CHECKS AND BALANCES

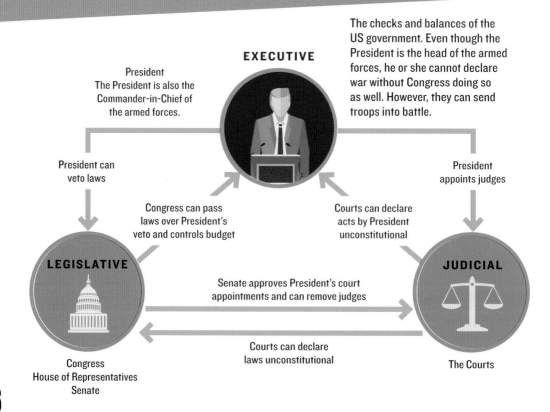

The checks and balances of the US government. Even though the President is the head of the armed forces, he or she cannot declare war without Congress doing so as well. However, they can send troops into battle.

EXECUTIVE

President
The President is also the Commander-in-Chief of the armed forces.

President can veto laws

President appoints judges

Congress can pass laws over President's veto and controls budget

Courts can declare acts by President unconstitutional

LEGISLATIVE

JUDICIAL

Senate approves President's court appointments and can remove judges

Courts can declare laws unconstitutional

Congress
House of Representatives
Senate

The Courts

PRESIDENT'S ORDERS

While there are checks and balances in place, there are also powers that a President has, and no-one else can control:

- they can grant pardons
- as Commander-in-Chief of the armed forces, the President has access to the USA's nuclear arsenal via the 'Football'. This is a black leather bag. In it are the means for the President (after identification) to issue an immediate order for a nuclear strike. The 'Football' moves with the President; it is carried by security staff.

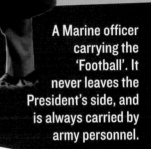

A Marine officer carrying the 'Football'. It never leaves the President's side, and is always carried by army personnel.

EXECUTIVE ORDERS

While the President cannot pass new laws, they can issue an executive order, which is legally binding and works within the existing law. Executive orders are issued by the President themselves and cannot easily be overturned by Congress. The only person who can reverse them is the next President. Executive orders allow the President to act directly, rather than going through the often lengthy process of gaining approval from Congress. However, all orders need to be constitutional, and can be legally challenged on those grounds. If an executive order is found to be unconstitutional, it will be revoked.

27

WHAT DOES THE FIRST LADY OF THE USA DO?

So far, every President of the USA has been male, and if they were married, it was to a woman. The President's wife is called the First Lady. She holds a very public position, but it is one that, for the most part, she can define for herself.

DURING THE CAMPAIGN

During the presidential campaign, a candidate's partner will often join them for events, and be publically supportive. Most recently, Bill Clinton attended events alongside Hillary and would talk to journalists in support of her. Melania Trump was less visible during her husband's campaign, instead focusing on taking care of their son, Barron. Trump was mostly supported by his daughter, businesswoman Ivanka Trump.

Bill Clinton joins his wife, Hillary, on stage during one of her campaign rallies in 2015.

MAKING A MARK

As soon as the President takes office, the First Lady sets out what her role will be over the next four years. Her offices are located in the East Wing of the White House, and she too hires staff to assist her. Many First Ladies in the past have been highly qualified professionals, bringing a huge number of skills to the role. Besides heading the organisation of events at the White House, the majority of the First Lady's work is associated with charities or involves setting up government initiatives. Michelle Obama, a lawyer, who was First Lady from 2009 to 2017, focused her efforts on children, education and veterans. Hillary Clinton was a ground-breaking First Lady in that she was the first to have her own office in the West Wing. She had a political career in her own right, and was elected senator for New York State while her husband was still in office.

Michelle Obama harvests vegetables from the White House garden together with local schoolchildren.

MELANIA TRUMP

Born in Novo Mesto, now Slovenia, Melania Trump (then Melanija Knavs) moved to the USA while she was a professional model, in 1996. She met Donald Trump in 1998, and the two married in 2005. This is Trump's third marriage, and her first. She no longer models, and instead mostly focuses on taking care of their son, Barron, who was born in 2006. She has never shown an active interest in politics and was initially not keen on her husband running for President, because she was worried about how it would affect their family. For the first few months of the presidency, she remained in New York with Barron. Both of them joined Donald Trump in the White House in June 2017. She has expressed an interest in initiatives to tackle cyber-bullying, but has yet to define her role as First Lady.

WHO WORKS IN THE WHITE HOUSE?

The White House is at the heart of the US government. It is not just the workplace of the President, but also hundreds of staff – both those who the President hires to help him run the country, and those who work behind the scenes throughout the White House.

PERMANENT STAFF

While President Trump was being sworn into office, the White House was a hub of activity. The biggest day for its permanent staff had come: the changeover of residents. Almost 100 maids, butlers, ushers, chefs and florists ensured that, within six hours, the White House had been prepared to welcome the First Family to their new home. They unpacked boxes, stocked fridges with the family's favourite foods and made sure all their needs were catered for. Throughout each presidency, the permanent staff of the White House are responsible for maintaining and taking care of all the First Family's needs. Security guards patrol the building and ensure that the First Family and staff are safe at all times.

The former White House florist, Laura Dowling, prepares the building for a state dinner.

THE PRESIDENTIAL WORKFORCE

The West Wing houses the offices of the President and important members of staff. These staffers are appointed by the President and some of the most senior members serve as advisors. The Cabinet is a group of 16 leaders of government departments and senior staff, including the Vice President. The President is very close to these people and may meet with them on a daily basis to ask for their advice. Other key members of staff who are close to the President are his aides, including the Chief Strategist and the National Security Advisor, and the Press Secretary. He or she is based in the press office and is responsible for passing on important information and announcements to journalists, so that they can inform the public.

WHO'S WHO IN THE WEST WING

Trump's staff at the beginning of his presidency

CABINET-LEVEL OFFICIALS

UN Ambassador
Nikki Haley

Small Business
Linda McMahon

Budget
Mick Mulvaney

Trade
Robert Lighthizer

Environment
Scott Pruitt

Chief of Staff
Reince Priebus

THE CABINET

State
Rex W. Tillerson

Homeland Security
John Kelly

Commerce
Wilbur Ross

Treasury
Steven Mnuchin

Labor
Andrew Puzder

Defence
James Mattis

Health
Tom Price

Justice
Sally Yates

Housing
Ben Carson

Interior
Ryan Zinke

Transportation
Elaine Chao

Agriculture
Sonny Perdue

Energy
Rick Perry

Veterans
David Shulkin

Education
Betsy DeVos

OTHER SENIOR POSITIONS

Vice President
Mike Pence

Chief Strategist
Steve Bannon

National Security Advisor
Mike Flynn

Press Secretary
Sean Spicer

THE TRUMP TEAM

Trump started appointing his team shortly after he was elected President. There have been mixed reactions to his choices, and a number of concerns have been raised over particular members of staff:

- Former Chief Strategist Steve Bannon used to be the head of the news site Breitbart, whose journalism is known to be far-right, discriminating against women, immigrants, the LGBTI community, Jewish people and ethnic minorities.
- Education Secretary Betsy DeVos was heavily criticised for having very little insight into the state education system of the USA.
- The appointment of Attorney General Jeff Sessions caused concern because he has been accused of racist behaviour in the past.
- Former Press Secretary Sean Spicer was repeatedly criticised for his attitude towards the media and his many missteps at press conferences.

- The former National Security Advisor, Michael Flynn, resigned after 23 days in office when it became clear that he had misled the Vice President about contacts with Russian officials
- The head of the Environmental Protection Agency, Scott Pruitt, is sceptical of climate change and has sued the agency 14 times in the past, vowing to shut it down.
- Communications Director Anthony Scaramucci was removed from his post within 10 days, following a series of profanity-laden statements about then Chief-of-Staff Reince Priebus.

Of 16 Cabinet members, eight are climate change sceptics, and of all the staff working closely with the President, only just over half have previous government experience. About 14 per cent of Trump's team are billionaires, while only 0.00001 per cent (400 people) of the US population are.

Former Press Secretary Sean Spicer was criticised regularly for making inaccurate claims in defence of President Trump. ▼

THE FIRST DAUGHTER

Donald Trump has decided to appoint members of his family as his advisors, too. This is an unusual move, compared to previous Presidents of the United States. Trump's daughter Ivanka was instrumental in the election campaign; since Trump has been sworn in as President, she has accompanied him to important high-level meetings and events, although at first she did not have an official role. Since March 2017, she has taken on the position of Senior Advisor and now has her own office in the White House. She does not receive pay, because, as the daughter of the President, this would be against the law.

FAMILY AFFAIRS

Ivanka Trump's husband, Jared Kushner, is also an official (unpaid) aide to the President. Both he and his wife hold unique positions that were created by Trump; neither of them have a previous career in politics, but they are both highly valued by President Trump and are often consulted on sensitive and important matters. However, in May 2017, Kushner became subject to the investigation into Russia's interference with the presidential election, as well as his business affairs. The investigation has also focused on Trump's son, Donald Trump Jr, who appears to have met with Russian officials during the election campaign. Meanwhile, Ivanka Trump has been heavily criticised for using her current position to further her business interests.

'First Daughter' Ivanka Trump and her husband, Jared Kushner.

WHY ARE THE FIRST 100 DAYS SO IMPORTANT?

As soon as a new President takes office in the USA, they are being measured – against their promises and against previous Presidents. After the first 100 days, people take stock of the President's achievements and failures, as well as his popularity, and try to assess what this means for the rest of the term.

WHY 100 DAYS?

At the start of a new term, a President is at their most popular – the people have great hope, and Congress is very willing to cooperate in order to help him or her achieve their political goals. This is sometimes called the 'honeymoon effect' – it's a fresh relationship and everyone is happy to put their trust and support behind their new leader. The effect usually wears off after about three months, which is why journalists and commentators focus on those first 100 days and assess the President's work during that time. If done well, this first and important phase of a presidency sees a flurry of activity – bills are passed and executive orders issued.

HAS TRUMP FULFILLED HIS CAMPAIGN PROMISES?

During his campaign, Donald Trump released a promise: a list of issues he would address during his first 100 days in office. So how did he fare on the ones that were central to his campaign?

Trump points out and shouts at what he calls 'the dishonest media' during an event marking his first 100 days in office.

1 "MUSLIM BAN" — PARTLY SUCCESSFUL

On 27 January 2017, President Trump signed an executive order banning travellers from seven Muslim-majority countries from entering the USA for 90 days. The countries were Iraq, Syria, Iran, Libya, Somalia, Sudan and Yemen. The ban took immediate effect, affecting travellers who were already on their way to the USA. There were no exceptions to the ban, and it even included those who had a right to live and work in the USA. Trump supporters welcomed the ban, and saw it as a President sticking to his word and being a strong politician.

However, the order caused serious problems and was widely criticised. It caused chaos at international airports, as the people affected were held at customs and all had to phone for lawyers to represent them. It was criticised by politicians (including Republicans) and the public, because it was seen as a form of religious discrimination: people were banned from entering the USA because of their religion. Lawsuits were filed against the state immediately. Sally Yates, the Attorney General at the time, said she could not defend the bill, as she didn't believe it followed the Constitution. The bill was put on hold. Shortly afterwards, Donald Trump fired Sally Yates.

On 30 June 2017, a modified version of the ban was approved. People from Syria, Iran, Libya, Somalia, Sudan and Yemen were banned from entering the country unless they had close family ties, were permitted to live and work in the USA or were in education there. All refugees were banned from entering the country for 120 days.

Protestors against the travel ban in New York City. The city's mayor, Bill DeBlasio (not pictured), was joined by thousands of citizens to stand with the Muslim community against the discrimination of the executive order.

2 OBAMACARE REPEAL — FAILED

One of Barack Obama's signature achievements was his healthcare act, also called Obamacare, which aimed to ensure that people of all incomes could access healthcare insurance more readily. Trump and the Republicans believe the act needs to be replaced. Within the first 100 days, there was an attempt to redraft the healthcare act, but it failed. At the time, Trump remarked 'Who knew that healthcare could be so complicated?'. On 28 July 2017, the Senate voted against the proposed replacement of Obamacare.

3 THE MEXICAN BORDER WALL – IN PROCESS

Throughout his campaign, one of the staple promises Trump declared, and one that was hugely popular among many of his supporters, was to build a wall along the US border with Mexico. The reasoning was that this would stop unregistered immigrants from entering the USA; Trump backed this up by claiming that Mexico sent criminals over this border. Trump also declared that Mexico would pay for the wall.

Trump issued an executive order on his first day in office to build the wall. Budgets and possible designs of the wall (including a more fence-like structure) have been discussed, but so far the only finance discussions have been ones where the US government fronts the entire bill. Mexico has refused to pay, and its President cancelled a meeting with Trump over the disagreement.

Parts of the USA/Mexico border that are easily accessible are lined by a high fence and patrolled by police. Trump plans to run a wall along the entire border.

4 DEPORT 11 MILLION UNDOCUMENTED IMMIGRANTS – ABANDONED

During the first 100 days, Trump's team made no efforts to follow up on this promise. Experts believe that the figure of 11 million is exaggerated, but regardless of the actual figure, it would be a very expensive operation. Instead, Trump has ordered a sharp increase in border control, and more hiring of border agents.

5 PROSECUTE HILLARY CLINTON – ABANDONED

Despite Trump firing up supporters at rallies with his claim that he would make sure Hillary Clinton was imprisoned, leading chants of 'Lock her up!', he abandoned this promise as soon as he entered office.

6 DONATING HIS PRESIDENTIAL SALARY – COMPLETE

After his first 100 days in office, it was confirmed that President Trump has donated his full salary for January, February and March to the National Parks Service.

Trump attends the G20 summit in Hamburg, Germany. Reportedly, Trump was often left out of conversations, and the summit was referred to as G19 by some, in response to the USA's retreat from the Paris Climate Accord, and Trump's international conduct.

7 WITHDRAWAL FROM PARIS ACCORD – COMPLETE

The Paris Accord is an agreement between almost 200 nations to tackle climate change together. Shortly after the end of his first 100 days in office, Trump announced his decision to pull the USA out of this agreement. Small-business owners in many parts of the country welcomed Trump's decision, as they felt it was to their advantage. However, many politicians and big business owners, such as Mark Zuckerberg of Facebook, stated that it was going to damage the USA. A number of mayors since have announced that they will continue to honour the climate change agreement, and the state of Hawaii even passed a law to that effect.

OTHER IMPORTANT ISSUES

1 FOREIGN POLICY

Forging and strengthening relationships with leaders from other countries is one of the key aspects of being President of the United States. During his first 100 days, Trump has been very outspoken in his opinions of both foreign leaders and their policies. Striking a tone very different from any of his predecessors, he has been frank, and in some cases aggressive towards his foreign counterparts. He has taken to Twitter regularly to either attack or praise a foreign government, making international relationships very public and – some say – less diplomatic. Trump has had public disagreements with North Korea, China, Iran, Germany, Canada, Mexico, the UK and Sweden. The countries affected by his travel ban announced that their relationship with the USA had been strained.

Trump ordered one military strike. In response to Syria's leader Bashar al-Assad using chemical weapons against civilians, Trump decided to step in and order a missile attack on a Syrian airfield. This was unexpected, but drew praise from both Republicans and Democrats.

2 RELATIONSHIP WITH THE MEDIA

Even before Trump's inauguration, his relationship with the media has been difficult and at times strained. He often states that particular news outlets, such as the *New York Times* and CNN, are telling lies about him. He has regularly tried to discredit newspapers and new channels, and his former Press Secretary, Sean Spicer, mirrored this attitude in press conferences. More often than during previous administrations, journalists have been excluded from briefings, and their questions have been left unanswered.

> **"** Don't believe the biased and phoney media [...]. The only quote that matters is a quote from me!
>
> • • • • • •
>
> **Donald Trump tweet (@realDonaldTrump), 28 May 2016** **"**

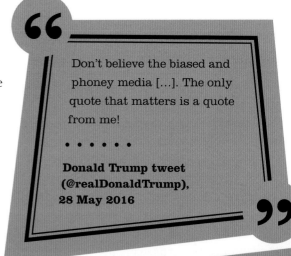

After Sean Spicer's successor, Sarah Huckabee Sanders, took over press briefings, the majority of them were held off-camera.

3 THE TRUMP TEAM AND RUSSIA

One of the most groundbreaking developments after Trump was elected was the investigation into whether Russia had interfered with the presidential election. This has already led to Michael Flynn, the former National Security Advisor, being removed from office. After the Attorney General, Jeff Sessions, also admitted to Russian contact before the election, he came close to being removed from office as well. This raised a new question: given that there was contact between Trump's campaign team and Russia, had the two parties somehow worked together?

The director of the FBI, James Comey, opened up a new investigation to try and find out whether Trump's team had acted illegally by working with the Russian government to influence the presidential vote. Shortly after his first 100 days in office, Trump fired James Comey. After changing his statement a few times over why he had done so, Trump said that it was over the Russia case. This has now brought the President's conduct into sharp focus, as it raises the possibility of him interfering with an investigation, which would be taken very seriously, if it proved to be true. For now, the investigation continues.

Russian President Vladimir Putin. Russia is considered untrustworthy by many Western countries.

SUCCESS OR FAILURE?

While Trump has managed to issue a number of executive orders and has addressed some of his promises, he has also struggled in his new role. The number of voters who still approve of him is the lowest it has been for any President in history. In addition, the Russia investigation, the 'Muslim ban' controversy and his numerous run-ins with foreign leaders have cast a long shadow over his presidency.

WHY AND HOW ARE PEOPLE PROTESTING?

When Trump was elected President, the people who hadn't voted for him were dismayed and deeply worried. More so than previous Republican Presidents, he stood firmly against most things they believed in, such as civil rights, gender equality, the safety of immigrants and the protection of the environment. So they decided to exercise their democratic rights.

FREEDOM OF SPEECH

In a democracy such as the United States, citizens have the right to freedom of speech. This means that they are allowed to voice their opinions, even if they don't represent those of the government. This allows people who are not happy with their government to engage in political activism – to stage protests and campaigns to try and bring about change, or at the very least, let politicians know they are not happy. This right is crucial, as it guarantees everyone a voice, and a right to be heard.

THE RISE OF US ACTIVISM

The Women's March, which was held the day after Trump's inauguration, was the first step many Americans took to show that they did not agree with their new President's policies and behaviour. Since then, there has been a level of political activism that has rarely been seen in the USA. People – many of whom have never been politically active before – are taking part in marches and rallies and are supporting organisations that are defending civil rights, such as the American Civil Liberties Union (ACLU). So far, the Trump administration hasn't acknowledged this movement as significant.

People protesting against Trump's proposed wall in Portland, Oregon.

FEB 2017

SUPPORT RALLIES

A tweet from Trump states that if all his supporters took to the streets, their rally would be 'the biggest of them all'. While this hasn't happened, many experts say that Trump has not just motivated his opponents to be more vocal about their political beliefs. Trump voters have been spurred into action by the heavy criticism of the President. They have formed movements as well, and are taking to the streets in defence of him. On 4 March 2017, 'Spirit of America' rallies took place in cities around the USA. However, with an average number of protesters at each rally of about 200–300, pro-Trump activism is far less significant than that of the anti-Trump side.

MAR 2017 Trump supporters at a rally in Denver.

41

ACTIVISM TECH

Activists in the USA are not just taking part in rallies; they are also making use of technology to coordinate and engage politically. Trump defenders have set up websites and social media pages that organise rallies and promote their agenda. Trump's opponents also make use of websites and social media, as well as apps. Their aim is to mobilise resistance that is directed towards representatives in Congress to get their voice heard where it can make a change to government. They are also working to ensure that the next elections have a high turn-out of liberal voters where it makes a difference.

5 CALLS APP

This free app alerts users to important votes in Congress that their representatives will be taking part in soon. It encourages people to take five minutes out of their day to make five phone calls to their representatives. The app offers a script for each call, so that users know exactly what to say to bring their point across accurately and concisely. It was built by volunteers, with the hope that as many Trump opponents as possible have an effective tool to protest and bring about a change.

CALL TO ACTION

This online application, similarly to 5 Calls, offers users phone numbers of their representatives, as well as scripts to use when calling. It too encourages users to have their voice heard by politicians and try to make a change.

Experts say that it is far more effective to call one's representative than to write to them.

SWING LEFT

At the moment, the majority of seats in Congress are filled with Republicans, who are highly likely to support Trump's agenda. However, a majority Democrat Congress could change this and potentially stop certain legislations being approved. It could also influence the likelihood of an impeachment of Trump (see pp. 44–45). The midterm elections, taking place in 2018, are seen as an opportunity to vote more Democrats into the Senate and the House of Representatives. The Swing Left website lists the 'swing states', where there are closely run races between Democrats and Republicans. The idea is to encourage people to enlist and help canvas in these states, making sure that as much support as possible is given to Democrat candidates there.

> " It's not something where once people go home from a march they go back to civilian life. This is people making anti-Trump activism part of their daily lives.
>
> • • • • • •
>
> **Ben Wikler,
> director for MoveOn,
> a group that organises
> activist events** "

The Capitol in Washington D.C. is the home of the Senate and the House of Representatives. ▼

WHAT IS NEXT FOR PRESIDENT TRUMP?

Donald Trump's campaign and presidency have contributed significantly to a divided country. His policies and behaviour have been uncompromising and highly controversial. Key members of his staff have already been replaced, and the investigations into his administration's links with Russia are gaining pace. The number of Americans who still approve of him is dropping rapidly. So what is next for President Trump?

MIDTERM ELECTIONS

At the moment, Trump enjoys a lot of support from Congress. The majority of representatives are Republican, and are mostly willing to give him their vote. However, this could change with the midterm elections. Should Americans choose to vote for more Democrats to enter Congress, Trump would have difficulty retaining the support he currently enjoys. It would be almost impossible for him to make any meaningful changes to the way the country is run.

A joint session of Congress, with representatives and senators all present. Of the 435 representatives, 194 are Democrat and 241 are Republican, while 48 Democrats and 52 Republicans form the Senate.

FIT FOR OFFICE?

Trump isn't just a controversial figure who splits opinions. On more than one occasion, he has misled the public. He appears to believe that anyone in government who speaks up against him or profoundly disagrees with him is in danger of losing their job. And the Russia investigations continue to reveal details of Trump's leadership style that could arguably put the country – or at least democracy – at risk. Should the investigation discover that Trump has acted against the law, he could face an impeachment trial.

WHAT IS IMPEACHMENT?

Impeachment is a process by which Congress votes on whether they believe the President can still be trusted. If two-thirds of the House of Representatives vote for impeachment, a further trial before the Senate decides whether the President should be removed from office. The Vice President would then take over the rule of the country until the next elections.

President Clinton (centre, with Hillary to the right) shortly after he was impeached in 1998; the Senate decided not to remove him from office.

THE CHANCES OF IMPEACHMENT

While the majority of representatives in Congress are Republican, an impeachment is not very likely. However, if this balance changes with the midterm elections, Trump could find himself in a more vulnerable position. In either case, impeachments are very rare. Throughout history, only two Presidents (Andrew Johnson and Bill Clinton) have been impeached, and neither of them was removed from office by the Senate. Although given that Trump is such an exception in US politics, it remains to be seen how he fares.

GLOSSARY

ADMINISTRATION – the people responsible for running a country

BANKRUPTCY – when a company declares bankruptcy, it means that the law has declared they are unable to pay off their debt

COMMISSION – to instruct a person or a group of people to do something

CONTRACEPTION – the use of physical barriers or chemicals to avoid getting pregnant

DETENTION – the act of keeping someone locked in a room or building

ETHICAL – describing whether something is morally right or wrong

EXTRAVAGANT – having no limits to spending money or using goods

FOREIGN POLICY – the political behaviour towards other countries

HACKER – someone who uses computers to access information that isn't meant for them

IDEOLOGY – a system of political ideas and beliefs

INCITE – to encourage someone to do something

LGBTQI – Lesbian, Gay, Bisexual, Trans, Queer and Intersex people

MANIFESTO – a set of policies, made public before an election

NATIONAL CONVENTION – the meeting of the members of a major political party, often to nominate a presidential candidate for an upcoming election

NOBEL PEACE PRIZE – an international prize, awarded for outstanding and important work to promote peace

PHONE BANK – a huge number of telephones; often used as short-hand to describe people supporting their chosen politician by phoning potential voters to gain their support

POLICY – a political standpoint

PUBLICITY – gaining attention from the media

SEXUAL ASSAULT – any sexual contact that happens without consent

SLUR – to make insulting remarks about someone

WORKING-CLASS – a social class of people who often have manual or industrial jobs

FURTHER INFORMATION

Here are some other books and websites that you can look at for more
information on Trump, as well as related and important topics:

BOOKS

Politics by Andrew Marr (DK, 2016)

The Presidents – Visual Encyclopaedia by Philip Parker (DK, 2017)

**Who Are Refugees and Migrants? What Makes Them Leave Their Homes? And Other
Big Questions** by Michael Rosen and Annemarie Young (Wayland, 2016)

Black History: Civil Rights and Equality by Dan Lyndon (Franklin Watts, 2010)

WEBSITES

https://www.whitehouse.gov
The official website of the Trump administration.

https://www.gop.com
The GOP is short for Grand Old Party – an alternative name
for the Republican Party. This is their official website.

https://www.democrats.org
This is the official website of the Democrat Party.

https://www.aclu.org
The American Civil Liberties Union's
online presence.

http://www.bbc.co.uk/newsround
The BBC's Newsround website is a
great source for news from around
the world.

INDEX